Like God in My Book?

DEANA PERRY

Illustrated by Windel Eborlas

WestBow Press books may be ordered through booksellers or by contacting:

WestBow Press
A Division of Thomas Nelson & Zondervan
1663 Liberty Drive
Bloomington, IN 47403
www.westbowpress.com
844-714-3454

ISBN: 979-8-3850-2146-8 (sc)
ISBN: 979-8-3850-2145-1 (hc)
ISBN: 979-8-3850-2147-5 (e)

Library of Congress Control Number: 2024905228

Print information available on the last page.

WestBow Press rev. date: 03/13/2024

WESTBOW
PRESS®
A DIVISION OF THOMAS NELSON
& ZONDERVAN

For Shawn and Boone, who are my
most precious gifts from God.

ဆဆဆ✿ααα

Trust in the LORD with all your heart and
lean not on your own understanding; in all
your ways submit to him, and he will make
your paths straight. (Proverbs 3:5–6)

ဆဆဆ✿ααα

Mama and Boone sat on the front porch early one morning while eating blueberry muffins and reading Boone's little book of Bible stories. The stories taught about God and how much God loves us.

As Mama and Boone ate their muffins, a bird landed on the bird feeder and began eating bird seed. Mama said, "Oh, look. The bird is having his breakfast too."

"Why?" Boone asked.

"Because he is hungry, I suppose," answered Mama.

"Why?" asked Boone.

"Because he has been working hard, flying around to build a nest and collect food for his family," Mama said.

"But why?" asked Boone.

Mama paused to think. "Because God created the earth and all the birds so they can fly in the sky," she said.

"Like God in my book?" asked Boone.

"Yes, like God in your book," Mama said.

And God said, "Let the water teem with living creatures, and let birds fly above the earth across the vault of the sky." (Genesis 1:20)

Daddy and Boone splashed in the water puddles on the sidewalk after a rainstorm one afternoon. The sun began to peek out from the clouds, and a rainbow stretched across the sky.

Daddy said, "Oh, look! What a beautiful rainbow in the sky."

"Why?" Boone asked.

"Because rainbows appear in the sky after a rainstorm," answered Daddy.

"Why?" asked Boone.

"Because the sun's light is refracted by water in the sky," Daddy said.

"But why?" asked Boone.

Daddy paused to think. "Because God made rainbows to remind us that He loves us," he said.

"Like God in my book?" asked Boone.

"Yes, like God in your book," Daddy said.

And God said, "This is the sign of the covenant I am making between me and you and every living creature with you, a covenant for all generations to come: I have set my rainbow in the clouds, and it will be the sign of the covenant between me and the earth." (Genesis 9:12–13)

Mama and Boone ran around the playground, swinging, sliding, and chasing. The playground was crowded because it was so warm and sunny.

Mama said, "Boone, watch where you are running, wait your turn on the slide, and say you are sorry if you bump into someone."

"Why?" Boone asked.

"Because it's good to be polite and respectful of others," answered Mama.

"Why?" asked Boone.

"Because that is what considerate people do," Mama said.

"But why?" asked Boone.

Mama paused to think. "Because God wants us to love each other," she said.

"Like God in my book?" asked Boone.

"Yes, like God in your book," Mama said.

Be kind and compassionate to one another, forgiving each other, just as in Christ God forgave you. (Ephesians 4:32)

Boone was helping Daddy rake leaves in the yard on a blustery day. As they raked the leaves into big piles, a strong gust of wind whooshed by and blew some of the leaves into the neighbor's yard. They continued to rake and collect the leaves in bags until there were no more leaves in the yard.

Thinking they were done with their work, Boone said, "Daddy, I'm tired."

"Whoa, not so fast," said Daddy. "We're not quite done. We need to rake the leaves in the neighbor's yard too."

"Why?" asked Boone.

"Because we should help our neighbor since some of our leaves blew into their yard," answered Daddy.

"Why?" asked Boone.

"Because it won't take long and we already have our rakes and bags ready," Daddy said. "But why?" asked Boone.

Daddy paused to think. "Because we are really raking the leaves for God and He wouldn't want us to stop working right now," he said.

"Like God in my book?" asked Boone.

"Yes, like God in your book," Daddy said.

Whatever you do, work at it with all your heart, as working for the Lord, not for human masters, since you know that you will receive an inheritance from the Lord as a reward. It is the Lord Christ you are serving. (Colossians 3:23–24)

Mama knelt by Boone's bed to say good-night. Boone was tucked in his warm blankets, and he snuggled his head into his pillow. As Mama leaned over to kiss his cheek, Boone saw a scary shadow move across the wall of his room.

With a soft gasp, Boone whispered, "Mama?"

Mama turned to look at the wall and said, "Oh, sweet Boone, it's only the shadow of the tree outside. Don't be scared."

"Why?" asked Boone.

"Because the moon is shining on the tree and through your window tonight. It's nothing to fear," answered Mama.

"Why?" asked Boone.

"Because morning will be here after your sleep, and the shadow will go away. Close your eyes and sleep," Mama said.

"But why?" asked Boone.

Mama paused to think. "Because God is here in your room to take care of you while you sleep," she said.

"Like God in my book?" asked Boone.

"Yes, like God in your book," Mama said.

> But the Lord is faithful, and he will strengthen you and protect you from the evil one. (2 Thessalonians 3:3)

One evening, Daddy sat quietly while looking at some old pictures of Grandma and thinking of how much he missed her. Boone was racing around the living room in his little red car but stopped at Daddy's feet when he saw the pictures.

"Daddy, where did Grandma Gigi go?" asked Boone.

Daddy answered gently, "Gigi passed away and went to heaven."

"Why?" asked Boone.

"Because she lived a long, wonderful life and now has a new home in heaven," answered Daddy.

"Why?" asked Boone.

"Because she believed and trusted in Jesus to save her and give her a home in heaven forever," Daddy said.

"But why?" asked Boone.

Daddy paused to think. "Because God loved us so much that He sent Jesus to save us and give up His life so we can be with Him in heaven one day," he said.

"Like God in my book?" asked Boone.

"Yes, like God in your book," Daddy said.

For God so loved the world that he gave his one and only Son, that whoever believes in him shall not perish but have eternal life. (John 3:16)

Boone came home from school one afternoon with a new toy car in his coat pocket. As Mama hung up his coat, the car fell out of the pocket. After dinner, Mama asked Boone where he got the toy car. Boone looked up at Mama and then looked down to the floor and said, "I found the car next to my friend's desk." Boone knew the car wasn't his to take, and he began to feel sad.

"Boone, do you know who the car belongs to?" asked Mama.

"Yes, Mama, I do," answered Boone.

Mama said, "Tomorrow you will give the car back to your friend."

"Why?" asked Boone.

"Because the car doesn't belong to you. It is dishonest to take things that don't belong to you," answered Mama.

"Why?" asked Boone.

"Because it hurts others when you behave that way. I am disappointed that you took the car. It will feel good to give the car back to your friend," Mama said.

"But why?" asked Boone.

Mama paused to think. "Because God wants you to do what is right. God forgives you for taking the car, and He still loves you," she said.

"Like God in my book?" asked Boone.

"Yes, like God in your book," Mama said.

No temptation has overtaken you except what is common to mankind. And God is faithful; he will not let you be tempted beyond what you can bear. But when you are tempted, he will also provide a way out so that you can endure it. (1 Corinthians 10:13)

Boone was helping Daddy put up the outdoor Christmas lights on a cold December weekend. Daddy realized he needed an extra string of lights so he got in the truck with Boone and headed to the hardware store.

Walking out of the store, Daddy saw a woman and a little boy huddled together at the bus stop. The woman and the boy were not wearing coats.

Daddy said, "Boone, please take your coat off."

Boone took his coat off. Daddy took his coat off too. Then Daddy gave their coats to the woman and boy. Boone saw Daddy talk to the woman and the little boy. Then he and Boone walked to the truck.

"Why?" asked Boone, once in the warm truck.

"Because it's cold and they didn't have coats to wear. We needed to help them by giving them our coats," answered Daddy.

"Why?" asked Boone.

"Because we have other coats at home, and they need our coats more than we do," Daddy said.

"But why?" asked Boone.

Daddy paused to think. "Because they are God's children and the coats we gave them are really God's coats. God wanted them to have His coats," he said.

"Like God in my book?" asked Boone.

"Yes, like God in your book," Daddy said.

Do nothing out of selfish ambition or vain conceit. Rather, in humility value others above yourselves, not looking to your own interests but each of you to the interests of the others. (Philippians 2:3–4)

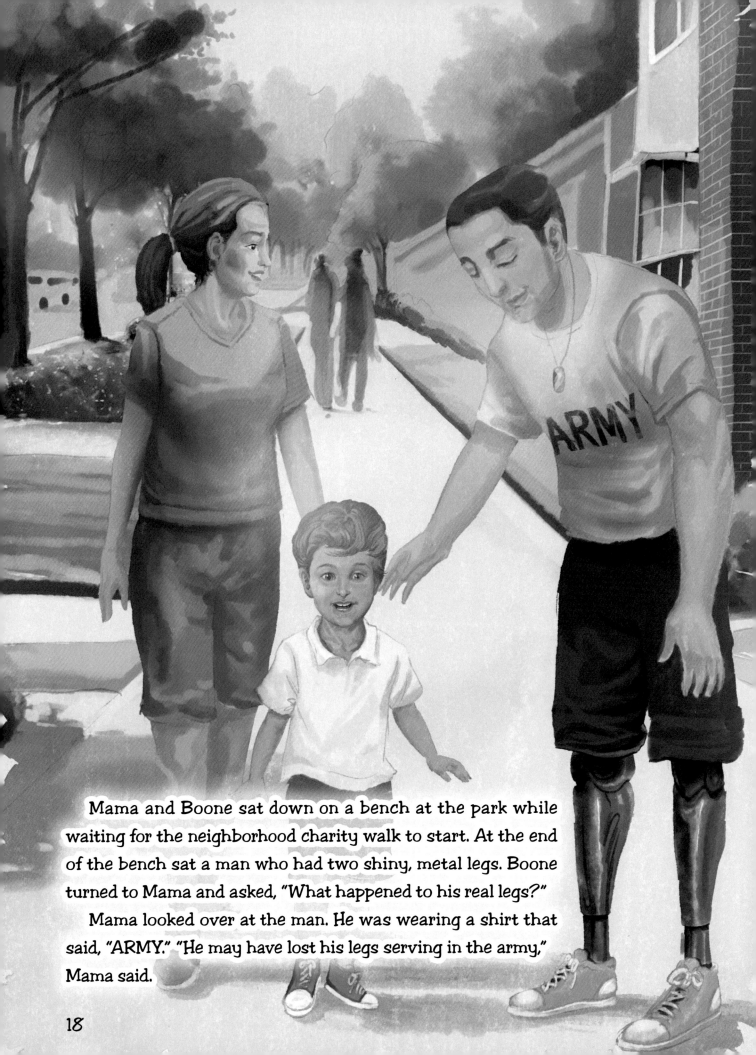

Mama and Boone sat down on a bench at the park while waiting for the neighborhood charity walk to start. At the end of the bench sat a man who had two shiny, metal legs. Boone turned to Mama and asked, "What happened to his real legs?"

Mama looked over at the man. He was wearing a shirt that said, "ARMY." "He may have lost his legs serving in the army," Mama said.

As Mama and Boone walked to the starting line, Boone turned to check on the man sitting on the bench. Boone watched the man stand up on his two shiny, metal legs and begin walking toward the starting line.

When the walk started, Boone had to walk fast to keep up with him. Boone asked the man, "Is it hard to walk without your real legs?"

"At first it was hard, but it's much easier now," he answered.

"Why?" asked Boone.

"Because I was weak at first, but I became stronger the more I walked," the man said. "But why?" asked Boone.

The man paused to think. "Because my new legs are stronger than my old legs, and God makes me stronger every day."

"Like God in my book?" asked Boone.

The man looked at Mama. "Yes, like God in your book," Mama said.

Even youths grow tired and weary, and young men stumble and fall; but those who hope in the Lord will renew their strength. They will soar on wings like eagles; they will run and not grow weary, they will walk and not be faint. (Isaiah 40:30–31)

After reading his Bible one morning, Daddy sat on the floor in front of the fireplace with his chin in his hands and his eyes closed. On his pajama feet, Boone slipped silently in the room and stood next to Daddy.

Daddy didn't move so Boone tapped him on the shoulder and said, "Daddy, I woke up. Are you still sleeping?"

Daddy opened his eyes and said, "No, Boone, I'm praying."

"Why?" asked Boone.

"Because I always start my day with prayer," answered Daddy.

"Why?" asked Boone.

"Because my days are always better when I pray. I ask God to help me make good decisions during the day," Daddy said.

"But why?" asked Boone.

Daddy paused to think. "Because when I pray, I am talking to God. I talk to God about everything. Talking to God reminds me to trust Him, thank Him, and listen to Him all day long," he said.

"Like God in my book?" asked Boone.

"Yes, like God in your book," Daddy said.

Do not be anxious about anything, but in every situation, by prayer and petition, with thanksgiving, present your requests to God. And the peace of God, which transcends all understanding, will guard your hearts and your minds in Christ Jesus. (Philippians 4:6–7)

Sitting quietly on the front porch one chilly evening, Mama and Boone were looking at the moon and the stars in the sky. The only sound was the rustle of Mama's coat as she wrapped her arms tighter around Boone.

Boone broke the dark silence with a sweet and confident voice. "Mama, God made the moon and the stars."

"Why?" asked Mama.

"Because God wanted us to have light to see at night," answered Boone.

"Why?" asked Mama.

"Because God is always doing things to take care of us," Boone said.

"But why?" asked Mama.

Boone paused to think. "Because I talked to God about it, and He said He loves me all the time, no matter what."

"Like God in your book?" asked Mama.

"Yes, like God in my book," Boone said.

Mama hugged him tighter and whispered in his ear, "Yes, Boone, like God in your book."

But God demonstrates his own love for us in this: While we were still sinners, Christ died for us. (Romans 5:8)

These commandments that I give you today are to be on your hearts. Impress them on your children. Talk about them when you sit at home and when you walk along the road, when you lie down and when you get up. (Deuteronomy 6:6–7)

Printed in the United States
by Baker & Taylor Publisher Services